Explore
CANADA

Jocey Asnong

RMB
rmbooks.com

We love this
wild and
wonderful land

Canada

Winter days are great with skates

Moose hike up high under summer skies

Newfoundland

St. John's

**Boats bring home
fresh-caught fish**

Fox leaps on red sand beach

Prince Edward Island

Charlottetown

Spring brings butterfly wings

Lobster loves to clack its claws

Nova Scotia

Our feet march to drummer's beat

Halifax

Dip our
toes in
ocean tides

New Brunswick

Squirrel steals a tree's sweet treat

Quebec

Hold on tight to our toboggan

Quebec City

Loon cries
as canoe
glides by

Ontario

Raccoons snoop through city streets

Toronto

Polar bears wear winter coats

Sticks pass pucks across river ice

Winnipeg

Families and flowers fill our fields

Saskatchewan

Turtles hide inside their shells

Mountains
stand tall
above ranch
lands

Alberta

Snow squeaks beneath our feet

Edmonton

There's fresh snow on ski slopes

British Columbia

Wait for whales to slap their tails

Sleep beneath the midnight sun

Yukon

Whitehorse

**Dogs race
over frozen lakes**

Caribou are on the move

Northwest Territories

Sky is bright
with northern lights

Yellowknife

Walrus shares arctic tales

Nunavut

Iqaluit

We ride by sled to visit our elders

For information on purchasing bulk quantities of this book, or to obtain media excerpts or invite the author to speak at an event, please visit rmbooks.com and select the "Contact" tab.

RMB | Rocky Mountain Books Ltd.
rmbooks.com
@rmbooks
facebook.com/rmbooks

Cataloguing data available from Library and Archives Canada
ISBN 978-1-77160-307-2 (boardbook)
ISBN 978-1-77160-496-3 (softcover)
ISBN 978-1-77160-308-9 (electronic)

Design by Chyla Cardinal

Printed and bound in China

We would like to also take this opportunity to acknowledge the traditional territories upon which we live and work. In Calgary, Alberta, we acknowledge the Niitsitapi (Blackfoot) and the people of the Treaty 7 region in Southern Alberta, which includes the Siksika, the Piikuni, the Kainai, the Tsuut'ina and the Stoney Nakoda First Nations, including Chiniki, Bearpaw, and Wesley First Nations. The City of Calgary is also home to Métis Nation of Alberta, Region III. In Victoria, British Columbia, we acknowledge the traditional territories of the Lkwungen (Esquimalt, and Songhees), Malahat, Pacheedaht, Scia'new, T'Sou-ke and W̱SÁNEĆ (Pauquachin, Tsartlip, Tsawout, Tseycum) peoples.

We acknowledge the financial support of the Government of Canada through the Canada Book Fund and the Canada Council for the Arts, and of the province of British Columbia through the British Columbia Arts Council and the Book Publishing Tax Credit.